The Dream

OrangeBooks Publication

Smriti Nagar, Bhilai, Chhattisgarh - 490020

Website: **www.orangebooks.in**

First Edition, 2022

ISBN: 978-93-92878-96-1

THE DREAM

SHUBHI SHARMA

OrangeBooks Publication

www.orangebooks.in

Index

Shadow Of My Soul

Fourteen years to go for my birth and the most I discovered in the world is to recognise who is " the shadow of my soul". I am not a good writer but I can explain this very well. I guess. The stories I am going to share is interesting and specific, full of fun details and sayings my father is known for. His words always paints a vivid picture of him and his telling stories. I cannot even notice an ungrammatical sentence in his collection of memories. But that doesn't matter, what matters is the stories and experiences to get shared in all that imperfect glory. Most people say I am just like my father both physically and mentally. We both have same mannerisms, facial expressions, thought process and an incredible amount of energy. From observing my father's behaviour and sometimes his lectures, I noticed he has influenced my choices and personality. My father is long, white and sweetest man on the Earth. My father was born on 26 june 1978 in modinagar UP. His childhood is full of antics and demonic situations. But soon his life became full of worries, money struggles, and also paying the bills and being responsible for his family. But he never lost hope and kept working to improve his family quality of life. At age of 28, he was married and at 29 his family was complete when I was born. Always asking about his life, I find some sadness in every aspect. My father has become such busy now that he has lost in his worries, sometimes like I am writing his biography to express my views on it. I often listen his stories from my bua. He was so naughty in his childhood that once he broke schools furniture. Sometime, he was so excited to keep sticks of different kunds and at time beaten with same sticks by my grandfather when he did some antic. We all are aware that according to Indian Culture, on being born as girls, people become sad or angry but in my case, my father was happy such that he gifted each nurse of the hospital 500rs and my grandmother was like- he has gone mad. Yes! This us true. He took me(a newborn baby) to a round outside while returning home scolded by everyone. He always wear high brands and also his legs are beautiful than mine. To say truth, a little jealous too. Only bad habit- he cannot live without his phone. Sometimes like throwing his phone from high. Big fan of politics-news and to see it he makes an excuse everytime saying it keeps him updated. Both of us are cancerian in nature- angry but trust me we never fought with each other. One more thing- this credit goes to me only but. I never gave him a chance to. He has hundred, thousands of friends. We have shifted from Modinagar to Rajnagar but our heart, soul, mind everything settle in our hometown only. He is the only person who understand friendship as a bond between two trust people. I told all about his past let me tell present too. My father is a purchase manager but after seeing his skills I wish of shifting him to sales manager. In this covid when people are left with nothing, my father willing to open a new business. With a pinch of hope to way of success he named it RAINBOW FURNISHINGS. His biggest support - his backbone is my mother. I heard all time that a father is a person who shows no emotion but feel it all time. And today while writing it I agree! I can see his dry tears in his eyes. The more I say about his life the less it is. I mentioned one thing- people say I am just like my father but the truth is that I can never ever be like him, he the one only because. At end I would just say-

The history is long
No future defined
One more hope for present
In every second of time
Never seen a man
With such experience
Positive in every situation
Sometime like a bit mysterious!
Fit and fine without a Gym
BTW- One more thing to tell that
I CAN NEVER BE LIKE HIM!!!!

The Roof

Day of Sunday, A girl went on the roof of a big house, all alone. Spend few hours over there and with the setting sun, she could feel the warmth over there. The scenery in front of her looks like a masterpiece. Then she heard as if her shadow was awake and asking her to turn around. She was scared for some moment, then she turned- seeing an unknown one she was shocked. Now and then she tried to run. As the setting sun was there, it started chasing her. With her scary expression, she went into the forest just in front of the house. Everyone warned her, not to go there. That place was dangerous. Then one came in front of her- giving her sympathy, not to worry just follow me and you"ll be safe under my control. It makes her walk on the cactus and she knew that she was hypnotized. Then the spell broke, and she awoke again. She ran faster there and screaming for someone to help. Did she go to the top mountains or valley low? Wondering, she fell on the ground- founding herself on the same roof she was some hours before. She wonders what happened just but she could not get it. After years another girl went on the same roof- all along and once again lost.

I Found God

God is great
Everyone's mate
Nothing is impossible
If he's there then life is stable.

Midnight, while reading my posts I found an idea of why not telling you the most strange moment when a soldier saw god .

Once , a soldier returning from war disappointing that he lost and now his country is in danger. He went straight away to a temple begging god to save his country. Pardoning god spent couple of months praying him like this when one day he realized that with a silver gate, a home was waiting for him carrying an old woman. He rushed to his house. Rang the doorbell and his mother came stumbling opened the door and went back. The soldier was in a shock seeing that and his mother sat on the chair like any another ordinary day. That moment was such when he noticed two things in gap of seconds. One , that his mother was crying quietly and second he saw God behind her , face angry and the phase he realized that he made a mistake or foolishness hence God wasn't listening to him since months. He huged his mother crying and put his head on her lap. Mother was also mom and then she gave her a blessing that another war the soldier was too alive and his country too. He defeated the enemy.

Now I must tell neither maybe this is a true story nor I have ever experienced such. Just convey a message to all my dear friends, pls don't ever make your mother cry as one droplet from her eyes, your whole world will be flooded.

To all mothers

Mothers are super

Also spicy as pepper

Mumma real God is in you

And we all children are not even belongs under your shoe...

SALUTE TO ALL SUPER-DUPER MOMS !!

Killer Heels

They disgust us, they terrify us, they fascinate us. There they shouted- once again the dead body is there- throat silt, wrists bound with thick black cable and air conditioner running on high. The cops are baffled. They once again found nothing- no fingerprints or DNA. People are in a state of panic. Over the past 3 months, around 58 people have been dead until now. They say, surely the murderer is a lady. Why? Because she is doing it for a quite long time. The heels over there. Once again a pair is there. Yes, a lady is a serial killer. One said- Do you have a history of violence? Others replied- I am a pacifist. I am tired of being a cop. I cannot read a mind of a serial killer?. Mr. Dawnson had to be called. Sir, you seem distracted replied Lisa. I am not able to understand what she wanted- you are also a lady Lisa, any idea why is she doing it? One girl mysteriously entered the door. Hey, who are you? I am who that does not matter, what matters is that she is a reflection of a monster. Before Mr. Dawson could do anything she left. Thinking about her for a while, he found a clue- the heels!.

He searched history- nothing be found. Last summer- replied Lisa- sir last summer 78 teenagers were killed in a whole month. After college started they started calling her "Killer Heels". As now a pair of heels was there near the dead body. Then after killing 78, she left the town of Derry and she now came here. No one is able to understand why is she doing it? They say- she walks at night- Toc-Tik-Toc, looks beautiful but as she comes closer, meow! Hehehehe? There the black cat cuts the way and Ohh! One more died. And she disappears. One more case shut and closed, family stunned, cops confused and cries are all around. After 5 years, one thing disclosed, a psychiatrist of the town said- she is inside, not there, she is everywhere and saying this the psychiatrist died the next second with eyes wide open, mouth open and just behind a little girl, he pointed her. When the little girl said- one more finished- have a good sleep doctor! Bye hehehehehe!

After minutes, the girl disappeared laughing and crowded all over. Mr. Dawnson started an investigation and Lisa was confused. Sir, what is happening? This is awful. She killed him so badly. She is heartless. Stay calm Lisa, Mr. Dawnson replied. I think we have to think of something differently. Mr. Dawnson along with lisa travelled around the world to find the history behind this girl. Though they found nothing. To take some rest, they entered a village named-sarak. The village was so beautiful and full with trees and all-natural facilities. They asked the people of the village some food but some shut the door in front of them while some ignored it. At end of the village, an old man offered them Place to rest and a bowl of rice, some veggies and tasty healthy foods. Mr. Dawnson asked- 'Kaka! This village is so beautiful yet no one is happy here'. The old man was quiet for a while then he spoke- 'son, this is a place of death, she has caught you in her eyes, she every day comes at night, says nothing to us but spread blood on each child's head.

Then she leaves.' Lisa was scared for a while yet she didn't notice it much. Time passed and every person shut their doors and went inside. All was lonely and scary dark. Mr. Dawnson said-' kaka, thank you so much for feeding us with your blessing, can we stay here for a day as well? Kaka agreed. The next morning someone from the window of kaka's house screamed. "Everyone come here". What they saw was strange. Kaka was dead, Mr. Dawnson was injured very badly and Lisa was barely breathing. They took Lisa and Mr.. Dawnson to the hospital. Mr. Dawnson murmured- 'this can't be true, all a lie, Oh Jesus please help me. And these were the last words he said. Yes, Mr. Dawnson was dead and lisa still survived.

Lily was questioned about the night. Shivering lily was so scared that she didn't even utter a word. After 2 hours she said- I don't know, she came and killed the old man, I was so scared I sat in a corner. Saying this lily got a heart attack and was rushed to the hospital. My Jesus! What is happening, Doctor knocked on the door and asked - Who are you, and how are you related to Lily? I am John, the new investigator of the case and I regret Mr. Dawnson died. Can I meet a lily doctor? Not now, Will update you once she's fine.

After 2 days, lily was awake and questioned-

Where am I? I am confused, Ahh! My head is hurting! May I come in lily? Mr. John sorry I will not help you, leave me alone. The door was closed and lily was questioned. Lily got an attack and changed into Taylor. It was a secret no one knew, lily had a split personality disorder. Taylor said- leave else will kill you. Mr. John started- 5 Sept 2008, you killed 5 boys from the hostel, I was one of them and anyhow survived. I followed you and found you were sitting alone in the woods and numbering something. Though I wasn't able to hear anything. The next day you disappeared. I searched for you for years and finally saw you the day before yesterday in the village. Come one now tell me why you did this?

Mr. John was shooted by Taylor. He died at the same moment. And lily was also shooted on the middle of the forehead.

A noise to be heard- Tomorrow's breaking news be- Killer Heels case finished. Both killer and investigator killed each other!

YET I AM STILL ALIVE…

Not Pretty Enough

Rose, a grown-up girl who lived with her mother in the town of Floral. She always wanted to be an actress so she decided to take a college for that.

On the admission day- Hello sir, said rose-' I want to be an actress and want training from you.

The director was busted- Oh! You just look at yourself. You are good but we want the best. Now get out!

Rose, went out crying heavily. After a few months, she decided to take a job as a product selling sales girl. She was ready to take up a job but again one thing was missing- she got a taunt again' Lady, you aren't pretty enough, our customers want someone more attractive. Try next time

Every time, each time and forever she was rejected saying- Lady you aren't pretty enough!

Rose tried everything to look beautiful but all she got was a failure. Like that there was an evening-

Hon! What happened you are looking upset? Asked her mom!

Nothing much mom replied Rose looking at the flower pot.

Okay then, come on have something to eat.

Next morning-

Mum! I will be late, going to an interview and then I will visit dad. Hope for the best.

Ok, hon! Take care.

Happily, this time Rose got the job of cleaning the mall, I.e. the cleaner (maid)

It was decided that Rose would lie to her mom about the difference between a maid and a salesgirl.

Yeah! Very sad. Now let's go to her dad-

At the Graveyard

In front of a coffin- rose sat quietly first then spoke- Hi dad, I finally got a job. I am lying, mom. Pls, don't tell her. Here, your favorite white flowers. I wish I would be as beautiful as they are. Anyways Daddy misses you.

The same evening her mom awaited her with a special dinner in happiness that she finally got the job after all failures.

Rose entered her house, looking famn beautiful and her mother said-

Hon! So proud of you, you finally got someone who looked at your soul, not your face. Anyways go get a bath and then will have dinner.

After 1 hour, her mother knocked on the bathroom door but there was silence. She again knocked more fastly- Hon! Come out I am stressed. But again a pin drop silence.

She finally broke the door and was shocked at the sight. The bath was overflowing the floor and the water was tinted red. She walked inside and screamed- seeing her little girl lying there with all cuts on her face and wrists. She burst out crying when something caught her eye. Taped to mirror a note- It read

Sorry Mum

I am not pretty enough!

The Dream

Chapter 1- Illusion?

October 19, 2019, the dusk of night crept. The moon light glistened onto the surrounding in the house, and we find a family having dinner. A couple and their beautiful daughter.

ALVIS- The father

AMARA- The mother

CARINA- The daughter

Suddenly, the doorbell rang. Opening the door there was a sudden sound like a huge, viscous bubble busting causing a hole in the sky. Though Amara didn't notice it much because a wedding was going in the town. The family went to sleep.

Next Morning-

Amara woke up and found carina wasn't in her room. She started looking for her in the whole house. All she saw was unbelievable! OMG, she screamed. She saw carina was all red handed carrying a bloody head in her left-hand moving closing to her mom. Mommy! I finished him, now you are safe and BOOM! Carina disappeared and OH, Amara woke up with a horror dream in the very morning. The day went like the normal one, but Amara can't forget the dream. All she saw was her little princess committed a crime. Mumma, can you give me something to eat please. It was another time Amara was daydreaming about her daughter carina. Anyways, the day went normal and the time, Alvis came home, screamed seeing his wife murdering carina's favorite teddy, he screamed loud, and Amara went towards him crying . I didn't do it honey! It happened, I am sorry, I am sorry. Where's my carina, asked the angry Alvis. She went to sleep, replied Amara. Confused and scared Alvis went to a psychiatrist the very next morning. Fixed an appointment and phone rings- the neighbor lady, Mr. Alvis come home quickly, your daughter murdered my dog and oh! One more dream in the early morning. Oh, my Jesus, what is happening to me? Confused Amara couldn't find out what's wrong with her. All she knew was her daughter committing crimes in her dream. Okay!

Days went like that. Then one day,

No knock on the door, no ring of the bell, only a message popping on Amara's phone, your package has been delivered. Though, the questions were she didn't order anything, still Amara opened the door found a big box, her daughter crying and screaming from inside the box. Amara rescued Carina and was so scared, that she again woke up with a bad daydream. The day went and the family had a good dinner, slept early.

Next Morning:

Mumma wake up, Mumma! What happened carina, why you awake so early? Mumma the boy down the street of Derry, caught red handed doing robbery and will now be hanged out in prison. Saying this carina, went to sleep again. Amara understood she was dreaming and slept again. But the morning, Alvis noticed the breaking news coming "A boy caught red handed doing robbery, will he be prisoned or will be hanged? Seeing this Amara was so shocked and terrified that how this news came true. Muddled Amara can't find out the thing and OH! It's such a rush to see them and know their time is numbered! Carina was mummering this sentence again and again sitting on her couch seeing outside the window. Mumma I can see all the dreary depressions of reality shown up to ruin all the fun. Huh? Carina what are you saying, carina wake up darling! Shhh! mommy, listen to me, the real fun is when the auras venture into the red end of the spectrum, though. Every now and again I'll see someone who's basically a walking stoplight. Those are the ones who get murdered or kill themselves. It's such a rush to see them and know their time is numbered, right mommy? Amara was so agitated, she called Alvis and asked him to come home quickly. Alvis knocked the door and both Amara and Alvis saw what their daughter was mummering- a widow. She'd murdered her two children by giving them each a cup of poisoned milk before bed. Then she'd hanged herself. Hearing this Alvis quickly did an appointment with a famous psychiatrist. Both of them took carina with them to the hospital. All tests began but the most unexpected thing was that all tests were normal, and carina was all fine mentally. This made Amara and Alvis to think what's wrong with carina? They first thought maybe a spirit possessed their daughter opposite the house, but it was all nonsense because the house was a happy home, with a big happy family. Then, why were those words, Ughhhh! Amara, please wake up, why were you shouting, what happened Amara? It was a dream? It was a dream? Alvis, please save carina, she's in danger, please save her. Alvis consoled the crying Amara, reminded her that carina has went to her mother's house for a couple of days and she's perfectly fine there. On Amara's interpretation Alvis started the psychological treatment of their daughter carina. Though nothing was found in the reports. All the doctors were confused as well. As such one day, Amara sat on a bench in the hospital, tired she slept for a while and what she saw in dream was incredible. . I walked up to Mr. Quinn the guidance counselor and shot him in the face three times. He fell back into the gym, dead. The shots were deafening. We heard screams in the auditorium. No one could see us yet. Here in this dream, she saw herself and her little princess killing someone Mr. Quinn. She waked up breathing heavily and was so frightened, though she handled herself. This was noticed by Mr. Smith (the famous psychiatrist). He ignored the incident once but again he noticed something strange in Amara. While doing the checkup of carina. Doctor noticed a spell being said by Amara. Though he wasn't sure about it.

Same Night,

I am the most Holy and Righteous angel carina. I roam the Earth, disposing of evil wherever I find it. I kill the monsters you don't ever want to know about. I crush them completely so you can sleep at night darling! No one can hurt you sweetie, I'll save you, good sleep carina. Saying this, Amara went outside leaving Alvis and carina in the hospital. This all had been noticed by Mr. Smith. Hearing all the talk Amara did to carina, made the doctor curious what Amara is up to and started following her. He saw her walking up the streets down the river. And there he saw, Amara, talking to a drunk and hopeless man, stumbling to the garage, and starting the table saw, then slowly lowering his wrists toward the screaming blade and oh! My Jesus, he died, a suicide? Amara turned towards Mr. smith smiled, a creepy face slowly said, hell is full; the dead shall walk the earth. What about heaven? Then, she ran away. It was a night Mr. smith could never forget. He explained the whole thing to Alvis while Amara was busy with carina. Mr. Alvis, your daughter is fine, but I think your wife is mentally unstable. He explained the whole night to Alvis, startled Alvis couldn't believe the doctor's words and started panicking. The doctor asked him to see his wife, the way she talks to her daughter in the night with his own eyes.

The Night,

Both went to carina's room slowly, without letting Amara know anything. I've found your name in the wet cement, written in remembrance sweetie. But it was written in reverse. And from below. Do you know, what it means darling? You know carina, no one wants to die alone and nor will you! I am coming in an hour princess; be here I'll be back here. Then, both of them followed Amara secretly, and what Alvis saw was so flabbergasted. He saw, Amara mummering down the river, sitting alone - As I pulled it out, I found myself staring at a pair of eyes, pickling in formaldehyde. I've been watching the police peel away the drywall of my house for hours now. So far, they've found 142 pairs of eyes in little glass jars. The scariest thing is, each one was staring at me. Cradling my four-year-old daughter in my arms, all I could do was listen as the screaming outside the house got louder and louder, interspersed with sounds of violence and horrible, horrible wet thuds and the unmistakable echo of muscle and sinew resisting the force that was slowly tearing them apart. All was Alvis's thought beyond, he busted out crying there only, heard by Amara and she ran away.

Amara held Alvis hand tight and screamed, A final hiccough of a sob, and she falls quiet, her body relaxed. She doesn't even have time to realize what's happening as I twist her neck with a violent jerk, accompanied by a dry snap of a sound. She's dead before she can even slump down into my lap. The door is giving way, the furniture pushed back. I may be torn limb from limb while I scream, but at least my baby angel's safe from harm and fall unconscious.

Next Morning,

Alvis and the doctor planned to start the mental treatment of Amara secretly. The doctor gave Alvis some recommended medicines, to exactly know what Amara's up to and why she's doing all this. But a mysterious tragedy happened. Every time Alvis make Amara eat the medicines, he could feel something uncanny within him. Similarly, one day, Alvis fell ill. Mr. smith was called to check him up. The doctor asked Alvis, any change in Amara's condition? Alvis agreed but this was strange that if Amara is getting better than why Alvis is getting worse in the health? Why was Amara dreaming such way? Why carina had to suffer being still in the hospital? Let's find out!

Chapter-2 The Past Or Present?

It's been 5 years today; I wish my baby would get better and call me to come closer to her. Listen, get ready soon honey, we must leave to hospital. Are you sure Alice? Every single day you dreamt like that; I don't know who cursed our daughter that her condition is such worse. Being a father, I am not able to do anything for my baby. Oh Jesus, it's better you curse me and save my Amara! Don't say like that Charles, may God bless our Amara to be happy and safe.

At The Hospital:

Mr. john, any improvement? Any movement or anything else? I am sorry to tell Mr. Charles, I never saw a case like that, no movement, the body is such like a living dead body. Jesus has just made her breath going on otherwise, I don't know how she is surviving, sorry Mr. Charles, I had to leave I have an operation, excuse me! Oh, my Amara, why you are still on bed. Get up baby, see I have brought your favorite ice cream, get up eat it dear, get up Amara, pls honey get up! (Crying heavily) Charles, ask your princess to get up, this isn't the time of sleeping, tell her to get up Charles, pls get up. Stop it Alice, have faith in God, he's there to help our Amara. He will guide my daughter to right path, she will get up soon. Don't worry Alice, stop crying.

At Home:

So, Mr. Charles, I am your doctor in hospital but here I am your brother-in-law. Now tell me brother, what exactly happened to Amara, you didn't tell me, 5 years passes still a secret. I am your family, trust me brother tell me, Alice, you tell me, sit here sister, tell me so that I can at least know the problem with my little Amara? What say, Charles, should we tell him. Hmm! It was 19 October 2014, around 5pm Amara was returning from office, she was so happy, she got promotion and after 10 days was her wedding, as you know. My baby was so excited, when an accident occurred, she was hit by two cars simultaneously. she got hurt a lot. You were in Austria that time, due to your special operation. My Amara was hurt so badly that she had a brain hemorrhage. 15 days treatment happened then; she went in Coma. Doctors tried hard for 1 year, each day, to get Amara's body in consciousness. but all the results were negative. No change since years and when you came back last year, we didn't tell you because we didn't want to remember that day again. 2nd year, doctors just told us that Amara can hear us and requested us to avoid any shock while talking in front of her, this would affect her. Then, her fiancée came in the room , his family broke the relationship with Amara, and it was the last time oh, my baby got a severe heart attack, we called the doctor and found, the shock affected her so badly that she now went to an imaginary world in her dreams. They told us, it's so hard for her now to survive. Now, she's just like as you are seeing. My poor baby, I don't know why my god has done this cruelty to a mother! I really miss her brother, I want to hear her voice, want to hug her tightly, pls brother make my dream come true, make my dream come true. That night, the family remembered some sweet memories with Amara. *now you all must be thinking, what is this? Well, all I showed you in chapter 1, was an imaginary world going on inside the mind of unconscious body of Amara. she has developed a life with the same boy and a daughter.*

Next Morning:

Sister, a famous psychiatrist is coming in our hospital today to take the survey of the patients. I had to leave, will see you soon, bye! At the hospital, the famous psychiatrist– MR. ENDREW, welcome sir, I am JOHN the most senior psychiatrist in the whole hospital. I am glad I met you, let me take you to all the patients slowly. After an hour, john took Mr. endrew to the ward of Amara. Seeing the still body, Mr. endrew baffled. He asked john about the patient and asked to take part in her treatment because in his 25 years of job, he never saw such case and was curious about her condition. Condition was clear, doctor john gave Amara all the medicines and tests were done. How could this be possible? Mr. john, the medicines you are giving are of high dose, they are consulted if a patient needs to remember anything but giving it in such huge dose makes the patient forget everything. No, no sir, it's just my hand slipped, and few drops are added extra, for the first-time sir. Relax!

Same Day,

Just an ordinary day, both the doctors started the checkup of Amara. john gave all the normal medicines he used to do and at around 9 pm, both left for home. Mr. endrew, its late night, you come with me to my home, we will take care of you. No no, doctor john that's perfectly fine, I'll book a hotel. Mr. endrew, it's just one night, come with me and will both have a good dinner and then some champagne. Otherwise, there's no time to spend together. We'll have some talks and experiences as well. The night was good and the whole family enjoyed.

Next Day At The Hospital, Alice Screamed:

Oh my god, a miracle, a miracle, Charles, john all come here. My baby, she's mummering something, oh my poor little Amara, do get up, Mumma wants you. Charles, hear carefully she's saying something. And this was such that the news spread in the whole hospital and then to the whole city. A hot trending news- a still body mummer, will she get up, will she be in good health. It was such that the whole city was now praying for Amara to get soon, she wasn't less than a celebrity now. This was the first time in history, a still body to become the hot topic for the city. Mr. endrew was called to hear the mummer words by Amara. After a three-hour concentration, endrew found something incredible. I know what it is, my god I know, the situation is clear john, I found the solution. But what's that Mr. endrew, what happened what you found out? Endrew took john to a library, and he showed him a book named- The psychological disease. It was a state where the person starts living in an imaginary world and thinks he is perfectly fine and his whole world is within him. It's a psychological brain disease john, it happens when the brain is affected because of an incident and is temporarily damaged. What Amara is facing now is that she's living in an imaginary world maybe with her husband and a child. You heard the words, Alvis, Carina, maybe that's her family, she wanted but you know she can hear us, she can feel the touch, she knows our presence around her, since last 5 years she's been living in an imaginary world. Because she was so busy with her family, the voice of Alice and Charles crying wasn't reaching out to her. Maybe she can hear it while sleeping. Let's go, I'll make you hear what Amara is mummering.

At The Hospital,

"My whole world sits beside you Alvis, me, my husband and my carina. This is the best family I have, I want no one else. I love my family". See john, what she's mummering is what she is seeing in dream, according to her, her whole world is within her made up family. You know john, this happens to only 1% among the whole population. I always wished to solve a case like that and finally got a chance to! So, sir, what we need to do now, I mean what is the solution. Begin a discovery, let's be the cops for a while. Hahaha, just joking, john I want to know more about Amara, can we have a little champagne tonight together? Of course, sir, why not, I would love it.

Same Night,

So, mrs Alice, what exactly happened to Amara, why she went in such state. Alice repeated the story, she once told to john- It was 19 October 2014, around 5pm Amara was returning from office, she was so happy..

....

....

.... My poor baby. Alice finished her story, and it was really shocking for endrew because in such sensitive cases, patient dies from a heart attack or another. But she was alive, that was appreciable. After having dinner, whole family sat in front of the television, the news was an ultimatum, the main topic was Amara, when will she recover, will she survive or die. Seeing all this, Alice busted out crying. Endrew told her to be brave, he will make Amara fit and fine like before. Now, Amara's condition was such that to solve it, was a passion for endrew, learning for john, blessing for her parents and mystery entertainment for the public. The study began, both the doctors used to spend nights resolving such case, what to do and what not to. As such **Few Days Passed, Then One Day,**

A huge sound like a bubble burst from Amara's ward, the glass broke, that means, she wanted to get up, then why sir, Amara didn't woke up, if her body became unconscious. This is because john-

Chapter 3- Found The Solution!

John, call Mr. Charles with her wife now. They all sat in the canteen and then endrew started- see, we all know that Amara is now living in an imaginary world, but she can hear us and feel our presence. We need to make such atmosphere in real life which she has dreamt of probably or in which she's living in now. What does that mean sir, that means we need to build up an Alvis and a Carina and make Amara realize and her husband and her daughter are in real life waiting for her to wake up and live in this real world happily. Because she can hear us, her brain will respond, and her body may respond. Whole family agreed to the plan and started to work on it. Whole family searched hard to make up a character as Amara was mummering. It was hard but as said since years, not impossible. The body was still no moving, it took the family months to find up a character same as Amara was mentioning. Then one day, finally I found them, sir a single father and her daughter lives in California. They both are quite poor, and his name is Ash, her daughter is Laira. They both perfectly match what Amara has been mummering by now. Ok, go get them John. Baffled parents broke in tears in the canteen saying- I can't believe, my baby is living in an imaginary world. My Jesus, he's so rude at these things. Calm down Alice, Amara will be fine, she will again get up and ask us to go make her favorite things. Be brave dear! The family and Mr. Endrew gathered in their house and asked the poor father and daughter to help. John made them understand the story and endrew for all they must do. Surprisingly or can say Jesus magic, they both agreed on working with the family for $3000 every day. All agreed, now

John took them to the ward and told Ash about Amara. confused ash could not believe that these things really happen. But it's all god's given.

Next Day,

The training started, ash was asked to call and force Amara to wake up. So did with laira. At first it was difficult but then as time passed, they both got trained and wished that Amara wake up. Then one day, a miracle happened. Reports found that Amara's body is recovering, she is now trying to respond. Her parents were happy that after 5 years, they went to church and thanked

God for his blessing. Time passed very quickly. Now both Ash and Laira began acting as a real husband and daughter.

Then one day,

Quick doctor, come here, the nurse shouted from the ward. John came running and asked the matter. Astonished john called endrew and then the family. What they saw was incredible. Amara, after 5 years first time opened her eyes, seeing the beautiful beauty of the world, she softly said, Mom! Happy Alice couldn't believe her ears and hugged her daughter tightly. She then began to respond regularly. One day, she tried to speak, one day she tried to move her hand and by this process in 1 month she was able to recover a lot. Simultaneously she tried to recognize people around her, her dad, her uncle, her therapist and of course Ash and Laira. Things were doing well until a call came to Ash of a job offer of around $68000 per month and he called a quit! Alice busted crying and requested him not to but ash became selfish and left with her daughter. Same day, when Amara asked about Laira, there was a silence. She repeated, but again a silence. Then the family took a decision of telling Amara everything, how she went in a imaginary world, how she felt, how the family was succeeded making the imaginary world true everything. But Alice opposed. Of course, any mother could do that, she didn't want, her daughter to get lost again in the imaginary world. After so many attempts of making Alice agreed, Endrew said- Mam, if we didn't tell her the truth now, she will be in coma again, knowing ash and laira left. Pls mam, it's the correct time of letting Amara know everything.

The Night,

All sat in the ward with Amara's favorite pizza and the cake. After the dinner Amara asked them, why all this. A silence for a while then endrew spoke, hi Amara today we all are going to tell you about a girl who went in an imaginary world for about 5 years. She was a cute, happy little girl who left her parents by lying silently in a hospital's bed for 5 years. First no one knew about her condition but then it was recognized that she's been living in an imaginary world with a husband and a daughter

....

....

....

....

....endrew finished the story. Amara replied- ohh it was quite bad, then then what happened. Then, the girl came in consciousness and was told everything by her parents. Then john said, you know it is a real incident happened with a girl. Eager Amara asked the name. a silence one more time, Alice started crying and Charles (his father) replied- it's you baby! A shock for Amara and she started laughing, nice joke dad, but seeing the serious faces of everyone left Amara disturbed and went to a silence for 2 minutes. Then john spoke, we know it's hard for you but understand Amara, you don't have a husband, none a daughter, but you have beautiful parents. I haven't seen such a smile on their face in the past 5 years on the day you opened your eyes. A trauma for Amara, she couldn't accept that she was... oh my god.... All finished and left Amara alone to think about the condition.

Next Day,

4 faces with a pinch of disappointment walked in Amara's ward and found she was alright, sitting on the bed having her favorite toast and salmons. Disappointed faces became cheerful ones and then Amara said- I was stupid, I thought about it all the night and found out after all of this, **I Still Survived Healthy And Fine!!!!**

The problems will come
With a thundering storm,
Stones under legs
Fire above the head.
With hands laughing,
Burning in fire.
We have not to be a shyier,
We have to be together.

With blowing air,
The blood spreading over here.
Of respect, Of disrespect,
Of head and Of chest.
Have to be born under problems,
We have to be together without being formal.

In light, In the dark
We have to mark,
In hate, In love
In loss, In a win
In every mark of life,
Bury our dreams,

We have to be together
In every bitter cream....

It's Better To Be Deaf

It's better to be deaf
Because nothing is left
That is to be hear
As, the world today left no dear
World is full of crime
Everyone thinks themselves as prime
Noone is safe overhere
Who is, a part of rare

It's better to be blind
Because nothing has been hide
The newspaper coming daily
Some come out of them only
Having no crime or low politics
Perfectly defined as Hailey's comet.

It's better to be dumb
At least not to speak
Speaking once means, whole
World to quarrel with.
No one is kind, in this world of crime
No one is soft hearted

When assault cases come, they are not even melted.
Today people have no heart , no brain
To feel that pain,
My Lord! Whole world is selfish now
We can survive in this how?
Help the world to be kind
Or make me dumb, deaf or blind!!

Let Me Taste The Rainbow

Let me taste the Rainbow
7 colours and bold
Each smell like
From wet mud a beautiful made pot
Few years ago, I was sitting by window sill
Quietly imagining what Rainbow tastes like
I desperately needs the answer
Knowing it may differ from person to person,
Hence I found my own explanation
The red tastes like strawberries, but looked like blood,
The orange looked like orange but tastes like candies glooved
The yellow tastes sour like sun
Green has an strange taste looked like lot of fun
The blue is salty as calm sea
Purple tastes like flowers and smells just like sweet tea
Pink has a flavour of soft marshmallows, like lots of balloons floating in air
Now I feel so much free
And know how exactly Rainbow tastes like

Now I feel so lazy...

LET ME TASTE THE RAINBOW

Fragrance Of Dirty Hands

Diamonds, Ruby are precious
Blue Sapphire is special
All difference is just
They look beautiful hence they worth
But we never noticed the real Diamonds
We have, all around the world
Each is dependent on them
They serving us for years
Asking no fee in return
This is an unusual love
Cooking-Washing-Cleaning-Building
To serve us they even skip their learning
All guessing who are they
We mould them like clay
Between roads of garbage
They live in severe shortage
They have Hemispam
Nailed arms with those dirty hands
Still, they create the scent of the fragrance

They are best
We just made the mistake of not recognising them
Teaching them their level
Never realized God
Because of them only we are properly settled
Foreigners are independent
They do everything themselves
At least we are lucky
While going to work or waking up
We get breakfast ready
House clean, everything set
And we say "yippie"
Ever thought about who are they
They are those labourers
Who serves us in a special way
Human! They are attackers none kidnappers
They are our that feel
Because of whom we have learnt manners
Once a year a day comes
To make us their unusual love
Friends make this single day worthy for them
We may do our work own
But trust me
No one can give us love diamonds better than them!

FRAGRANCE OF DIRTY HANDS

My Devotion

Shiva- the destroyer
The plethora of power
The synonym of destruction
He- who can never be defeated
The one who can demolish the world opening his third eye
The most vicious poison rests in his throat
Words are never enough to define whose eminence
The greatest manifestation of divine
The eternal and the auspicious
That Shiva the Ultimate God!

Lord- You are my force
Gentle as snow flake
You are my passion
Quite as twilight
You are my love
Free as singing soul
You are my freedom
Holding me soo close.

Truth is that, Godness and beauty are eternal trinity,

He is the quality of rarity and divinity.

According to my thoughts for the people who not trust him-

He may not be the truth

But the truth is he only

Shiv may not be beauty

But beauty is Shiv

Shiv may not stand for Goodness

But Goodness is surely Shiv

Now Let us all strive for trinity

Because truth is goodness of trinity and Lord Shiv is Beauty!!

The Cage Is Broken

The history is unfold
The books are opened
On the second last page there
The cage is broken
See, the rainbow colours
Flying in such a way
Birds have found
Their own ray
Freedom is expressed
As such a clue
The restriction is free
Just have to go through
The cage is left
With some meals in it
Finally it has got some rest
Let's relax a bit!!

O King Of Holy Sanctuary

O! Light of god! May I be graced by your benevolence
O god! May there be strength in my prayers
May god showcase my family a miracle
May he get to know about my suffering

The condition of my heart is obvious to you
We will bow down our heads and say
O king of holy SANCTUARY, you may
Look at us with eyes of benevolence

O king of holy SANCTUARY, help us, show us your excellence
The hearts of poor ones will also blossom
O Parton of poor! What will world say?
If I go back empty handed from your doorstep

O king of holy SANCTUARY
Prove that you are not less than awesome
My heart finds peace when your light shines
Listen to my request

There's no one is this world except you

Listen to my voice in these silences
My heart has called out to you
If you also wouldn't hear us
Tell me please where should I go then

O king of holy SANCTUARY
Give us blessing and happiness plus
Please remove the veil from your face now
Give me medicine to my pain

My life lies in your hands
Either eradicate me or make me
How will that one be tortured by grief of the world
The one who has a noble guardian like you
Listen to my call- oh my Lord
Before my eyes get drenched

O king of holy SANCTUARY
With eyes of benevolence
Let me introduce my life
Spreading a positive successful scent!

O KING OF HOLY
SANCTUARY

A Letter From Heaven

When tomorrow starts without him
And he's not there to see
The sun rises and everyone opens their eyes
All filled with tears for him
He wishes we all won't cry
The way we are doing today
While thinking of many things
I didn't get anything to say
He knew, how much I loved him
As much he loves me
And each time thinking of him
He knows I miss him too
But when tomorrow starts without him
Please try to understand my heart
That an angel came and called his name
And took him by the hand
She said- his place was ready
In heaven far above
And he had to leave behind
All those he dearly loves
But as he turned to walk away
A tear fell from his granddaughter's eye.

For all his life He always thought
'I didn't want to die'
He had so much to live for
If he's healthy and fine
It seemed almost impossible
That he was leaving
His granddaughter thought of all the yesterday's
The good ones and the bad
She thought of all love they shared
And all the fun they had
She thought if she could relive yesterday even for a while
That would be her almost wish of her life
Her grandfather would say goodbye and kiss her
Maybe seeing him smile
But then she realized, this could never be happen
Because emptiness and memories will take place of him
I swear I am full of sorrow
The granddaughter is me, I wonder
It is going to be one year on 4 October
While traveling to heaven my grandfather
Missed his home so much until god
Looked and smiled at him
From his golden throne
He said this is reality
Today is defined
Can't promise for tomorrow
All you can do is send a letter to her
Waiting for you on earth

Yet to come along
Hold her hand and say- I am worth
Here's a letter for you
Just to say at least
Dear Shubhi- I always love you.

I miss you dadu.

Wallpaper

The room was dank and dreary
The past hung in the air
There was a scent of mildew
A smell of history was there
The paint was old and faded
With stains all dark and brown
The wallpaper too was dated
And it needed to come down
It was a home for 50 years
That stood so strong and proud
It comforted all of our fears
Far from the madding crowd
We stripped away the paper first
Each layer a strip in time
It showed the old room at her worst
It really seemed a crime
To tear it down, and think of when
Each layer was first applied
The walls that seemed so tall again I just stood there and cried
I thought about the birthdays
Celebrated in this room

Of getting covered all in glaze
That we cleaned off with a broom
The roses were much redder
Than I remembered them to be
In fact it now looked better
Than it did when I was three
I remembered Mother loved this
And of how it made her smile
The next layer though was not as nice
"T was beige and a sort of lime
It made the room feel cold like ice
It spoke of another, somber time
I looked at the wall and I noticed the lines
Marking our heights as we grew
This was on a paper all covered in vines
Mom loved this one, we knew
It seemed surreal that Mom was not here
To see these passages pass
But we knew in our hearts that she was still near
As we looked at paper covered with Bass
That was from when Uncle Jim came to stay
And our folks gave up their room
To help out a brother who I still love to this day
One who can always help brighten my gloom
They changed the wall just for him
To make it seem more like it was his
They put their life on hold for Jim
And the wallpaper choice was his

The years pass by more quickly now
The paper doesn't change too much
Jim moved out and that is how
The paper changed just a touch
Mom got sick and Dad quit work
He did the room in flowers for our mom
It was at this time we noticed the rooms quirk
One of those things that made you go hmmm
Far up in one corner behind a section of curtain
Dad had left a small square showing the years
worth of papers we were certain
It was to help mom with her tears
Now as we finished we looked to the man
Sitting alone in the old corner chair
He smiled at us as best as he can
But I don't think he knew we were there
I handed him some paper and I looked in his eyes
He stared clear on through me
And then he started to cry
This was the last of this paper he'd see
Dad and the house now have gone into dust
The years get short and have tapered
But to go back in time I know all I must
Do, is look at my small square of paper.

The Mirror

The mirror, once a pristine silver surface

useful for the lucid view of one's own soul

in the years since passed since first unveiled

has become tarnished with the rust of others negative thoughts

has become cracked and broken with perceived fatal flaws

has been knocked over, thrown about the room

pushed through walls, stomped to the ground in fits of self-hate

colored black with the slow snaking ink of depression

the mirror, once a beautiful thing to behold

showing the true form of ones character

reflecting the gorgeous image of oneself (inside and out)

now has been reduced to an ugly evil device

tormenting all who gaze upon it and see themselves

writhing, squirming, twisted and grotesque a truly wretched form

for it no longer shows oneself as one knows thyself to be

but instead reflects the views of the outsiders, people known only to see

flaws, to be jealous, to hate, to want to destroy any beauty or thought

of self worth, confidence, those who hate themselves.

so a word from one whose mirror is broken
who does not know if he can mend and repair
you are beautiful
~ you are unique
~ you are special
~ you are loved
you are how you view yourself - so protect your mirror

The Legend (Narendra Modi)

A legend was born, to change the world
On September 17,1950, to pass every hurdle
He is a man of great sense
We respect it hence
His kindness and sensibility is overloaded
Saved people from being flooded
God created thousands of people
But he comes in a few
Raised from a small town of Gujarat
Common like all of us

But his mind is a masterpiece
His childhood was a bit struggling
Had to sell tea near the bus , Oh God!
Just because not to marry
He left home at 17 into a world deadly
He is a symbol of courage and strength
We all should be like him without any tense
Influenced by RSS, he learned spirit of

Selflessness, responsibility and dedication
After this struggle he got into politics
To change its history
To defeat all the country heads
Who were darkening the beautiful light shade
To become a mystery, for every common like us

Again he had to do struggle
Because everything around was puzzled
You might be thinking
Who's that I am talking about
You will get to know it soon
And realize the same , having no doubt
Okay! I give you a clue
With which you will stick like glue
He saved thousands of people
From different conditions
Sometimes drought or flood
Not let anyone spread his blood
Took revenge from enemies
With whom others were not able to do it for years

First a Surgical Strike
Which was up to high
Then an Air Strike , which he let it do very peacefully and light
Now you must have understood
You know one more, now he is working to let Bengal free

From a person so called "didi"
To make the country unite
He is trying hard
We can't even imagine how difficult it is for him

But still he's strong
As he know that he can't show his pain to others
If he let down
Then his country would never be awake
Would never be no.1
So , for his this hard work , he surely
Deserve a crown
That's why I said in the beginning
That a legend (MODI) was born to change the country , to change it's people.
For that Modi can be both a Beetle and an Eagle....

Thank you so much God for letting us meet such a masterpiece.

THE END…

www.ingramcontent.com/pod-product-compliance
Ingram Content Group UK Ltd.
Pitfield, Milton Keynes, MK11 3LW, UK
UKHW021644190726
13853UKWH00001B/50

9 789392 878961